HOW TO DESIGN YOUR WORLD

How to Design Your World

Hitesh Solanki

Copyright © 2025 by Hitesh Solanki
All rights reserved. No part of this book may be reproduced in any manner whatsoever without written permission except in the case of brief quotations embodied in critical articles and reviews.
First Printing, 2025

Contents

Dedication — vi
Acknowledgement — viii
Foreword — x

1 Introduction — 1
SECTION ONE — 4
2 Introduction to Part One — 5
3 What is the Vision — 9
4 The Power of Vision in History and Leadership — 15
5 Who am I? — 22
6 Redefine the Meaning of Success — 28
7 Breaking the Chains of Conformity — 34
8 Finding Your Voice in a Noisy World — 40
9 The Mirror Is Not the Truth — 47
SECTION TWO — 54
10 Introduction to Part Two — 55

11	Redesigning the Inner Lens	58
12	The Vision Within	65
13	The Seed and the Soil	73
14	Conclusion: The World Is Yours to Design	81
Book References		84
Recommended Reading For You		85

Dedication

To my beloved parents, **Mrs. Dhanbai Solanki** and **Mr. Devi Singh Solanki**—Your unconditional love and unwavering belief in me laid the foundation for who I am. You gave me the wings to explore the world and the roots to stay grounded.

To my wife, **Manjula Solanki**—Your boundless patience, silent strength, and selfless support have been the unseen architecture behind everything I've built. Thank you for gracefully managing our family while giving me the space to grow, without a single complaint.

To my children, **Himanshi** and **Eklavya**—You inspire me to dream bolder and build a future worth living for.

To **Hemsingh Patle** and **Manoj Sonawane**—Thank you for nudging, motivating, and reminding me to write this book when I almost didn't.

To my coach, **Mr. Rahul George**—For turning my thoughts into clarity and chaos into purpose.

To mentors and guides—**Mr. Sumit Agrawal, Dr. Meghna Dixit, Mrs. Pallavi Walia Raj, Cmd Bimal Raj,** and **Mr. Sunjay Chaturvedi**—Your wisdom, mentorship, and presence have profoundly shaped my growth.

With love, gratitude, and vision,
Hitesh Solanki

Acknowledgement

Writing this book has been more than an intellectual pursuit—it's been a journey of personal transformation. I am deeply thankful to those who have stood by me, guided me, and believed in me through it all.

To my parents, **Mrs. Dhanbai Solanki** and **Mr. Devi Singh Solanki**, your values, love, and belief anchor me in everything I do.

To my wife, **Manjula Solanki**, thank you for being my strength, shouldering responsibilities silently, and gifting me the freedom to chase this dream. Your grace under pressure has made this possible.

To my children, **Himanshi and Eklavya**, your curiosity and dreams fuel my own.

To **Mr. Hemsing Patle**, your push turned into my action.

Mr. Manoj Sonawane and the Bliss Books editorial team are needed to polish the shared raw thoughts.

ACKNOWLEDGEMENT

To **Mr. Rahul George**, your structured coaching helped me untangle thoughts and turn them into a meaningful message.

To the mentors who gave more than advice—**Mr. Sumit Agrawal, Dr. Meghna Dixit, Mrs. Pallavi Walia Raj, Cmd Bimal Raj, and Mr. Sunjay Chaturvedi**—thank you for your wisdom, truth, and generous guidance.

Foreword

We live in an age of unprecedented noise. Everywhere we turn, we are bombarded with messages telling us who to be, what to want, and how to measure our worth. From social media feeds to corporate ladders, from family expectations to cultural norms, we inherit visions of success and identity that often feel more like burdens than blueprints. This book arrives as both a mirror and a map.

As you turn these pages, you will meet Eklavya, a seeker whose journey mirrors our own. His questions are universal: Why do so many of us chase hollow victories? How do we distinguish between the life we've been handed and the life we truly desire? What does it mean to design a world that aligns with our deepest truths?

Hitesh Solanki does not offer easy answers. Instead, he invites you into a transformative process of unlearning—peeling away borrowed beliefs, societal scripts, and fear-based patterns to uncover your authentic vision. Through storytelling, reflection exercises, and actionable steps, this book becomes a workshop for the soul. You'll explore how perception shapes reality (Section 1) and how to consciously redesign your inner lens (Section 2).

What makes this work extraordinary is its balance of wisdom and practicality. Solanki draws from philosophy, history, and lived experience, yet grounds each insight in exercises that demand participation, not passive reading. You'll confront the "institutional paradox" (Chapter 5), dissect the "illusion of success" (Chapter 4), and ultimately learn to prototype your growth like a sculptor, one intentional stroke at a time.

To read How to Design Your World is to embark on a quiet revolution. The tools are here. The choice is yours.

Happy Reading!
Manoj Sonawane
Author of the book Learning 2.0.

1

Introduction

*****

"The world as we have created it is a process of our thinking. It cannot be changed without changing our thinking."
- ***Albert Einstein***

The Lens That Shapes Reality

Every day, we wake up to a world filled with choices, challenges, and opportunities. But how often do we pause to ask: Who designed this world? And more importantly, who is designing mine?

From the moment we are born, we inherit a way of seeing-shaped by family, culture, education, and media. These influences act like invisible lenses, filtering how we perceive success, failure, relationships, and even our own potential. But what if these lenses are distorting our vision? What if the world we see is not the only world that exists-just the one we've been taught to see?

This book is not about rejecting the past or blaming the systems that shaped us. It's about something far more powerful: redesigning our vision so we can live with intention, clarity, and authenticity.

The Two Architects of Your Life

There are two forces at work in every life:

1. **The Inherited Vision** – The beliefs, expectations, and definitions handed to us by others.
2. **The Designed Vision** – The way of seeing and being that we consciously choose, refine, and act upon.

Most people live by the first, never questioning where their dreams, fears, or definitions of success came from. They chase goals set by others, measure themselves against borrowed standards, and wonder why fulfillment remains just out of reach.

But a rare few pause, reflect, and ask:

Is this vision truly mine?

Does it align with who I am and who I want to become?

If not, how do I redesign it?

This book is for those who dare to ask these questions.

What You Will Discover

In these pages, we will explore:

The Power of Vision – How the lens through which you see the world shapes your reality, relationships, and sense of purpose.

The Stories We Inherit – The hidden forces (family, society, media) that silently script our lives—and how to rewrite them.

The Courage to Unlearn – Why letting go of outdated beliefs is the first step toward designing a life that feels authentically yours.

The Art of Intentional Living – Practical steps to align your daily actions with a vision that inspires, sustains, and fulfills you.

This book offers no quick fixes or rigid rules. Instead, it invites a deeper conversation, and many transformative questions.

Let's design!

SECTION ONE

HOW WE SEE THE WORLD

"Man is made by his belief. As he believes, so he is."
   -Bhagavad Gita (17.3)

2

Introduction to Part One

*****

*"The only thing worse than being blind is having sight but no vision."- **Helen Keller***

The Lens We Live By

Meet Eklavya, who was born into a tribal family and grew up in a small town. His parents were busy with their government jobs, so he spent more time around working adults than kids of his age. He lived in many places, studied at different locations, lived in hostels, travelled the world and worked with people around the globe.

He never felt fully rooted in one place. While being in two different worlds, one is resource-less and full of a connected community and sense of togetherness and the other with resources and full of opportunity but are struggling with loneliness, dissatisfaction, and stress, and they are behind a never-ending race. He kept on thinking about which world he belonged to and started observing, learning, reading, and watching them. Having conversations with people from different ages and cultures, learning about different beliefs, religious practices, and regional rituals, and talking about daily issues and why we do what we do. He viewed the world with a broad perspective.

Why do people feel unsatisfied even when they have everything?

The above question echoed in his mind as he recalled a businessman he had met in the city well-dressed, polished, yet with restless eyes that darted as if searching for something just out of reach. The man had a luxury car, a spacious home, a family, yet he had sighed and said, *"There must be more than this."*

Eklavya had frowned. *More than what?*

Then there was the elderly woman in the riverside village, her hands rough from years of work, her hut small, her possessions few. Yet when she smiled, it was like the first rays of sunlight spilling over the horizon, filling everything around her with warmth and quiet magic. She had laughed and said, *"The river sings to me every morning. What more could I need?"*

Two lives. Two ways of seeing.

One sees a problem, while the other sees a possibility of life.

The people from the above story are operating their lives through vision.

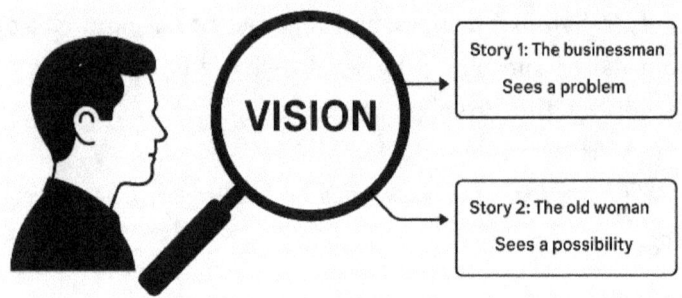

Figure 1: The Lens We Live By

Vision is a silent force that shapes how we see people, objects, relationships, systems, and even our own existence. Two people can stand in the same room, witness the same moment, and yet walk away with entirely different experiences.

Because the mind does not simply see what is in front of it. It filters everything through the layers of past experiences, beliefs, and emotions. These filters, woven over the years by family, society, environment, and even the silent memories, shape our reality before we even realize it. Vision is not something we are born with. It is something we build, sometimes with intention, but mostly without even knowing we are doing so. Here, the old woman and the businessman are operating their life with two different visions.

We see the pattern of the above story everywhere. The executives in glass towers, employees in cramped desks, and even young students hunched over textbooks. They have the same question. *What if I'm not enough? What if I never arrive?*

But then there is the cobbler under the banyan tree, humming as he worked, his hands moving with quiet certainty. *"Every stitch matters,"* he had told Eklavya once. *"Not because the world sees it, but because I do."*

The following questions arise as we proceed.

Why are we chasing careers, success, and recognition but feeling more lost than ever?

The answers weren't in grand philosophies or perfect formulas. They were in the way a fisherman mended his net, in the way a mother tucked her child to sleep. They operate the life through the vision of compassion.

That vision is not about eyesight. It is about insight, the courage to look deeper, to question, to unlearn, and live a life. It this lens (vision) through which you see life, and you can train it either to see problems or possibilities.

Let's learn about "what's the vision" in the next chapter.

3

What is the Vision

*****
"Vision is the art of seeing what is invisible to others."
- Jonathan Swift

That day, Eklavya sat alone near the river, under a tree older than the town itself. He wasn't doing anything just watching. Watching people pass by, each of them carrying their stories and decisions into their interactions with the world.

A child climbed the tree, giggling with the innocent joy of discovery.

A man selling vegetables tied his bag to one of the branches.

A tired woman sat in its shade and drifted off to sleep.

A young boy kicked the trunk for no apparent reason.

An older man folded his hands, bowed to it, and continued walking.

One tree. Yet so many meanings. Its significance changed with each passerby, depending on their needs, experiences, or even their emotions at that moment. That realization struck Eklavya deeply. We don't see things as they are. We see them as we are.

This thought lingered in his mind like ripples on the river's surface. If a simple tree could hold so many meanings for different people, what about everything else? How could I trust that what I saw was the truth, and not just a reflection of the filters built inside me? So what truly shapes our vision?

We often think vision is about seeing clearly. But clarity is an illusion. What we perceive is shaped by the layers we carry within. As we said it in earlier chapter that they are our memories, our fears, our joys, our culture, and the echoes of our past. Our minds are like artists, constantly creating patterns from every experience. Over time, those patterns harden into filters that frame how we interpret the world.

A raised voice might trigger the sting of anger, reminding us of painful moments when someone yelled at us. A compliment might feel like sarcasm, because we've grown up around people who never meant what they said. An opportunity might seem like a trap, burdened by the weight of our past failures and the fear of repeating them.

We all wear invisible lenses, built layer by layer from the life we've lived. And until we pause, truly pause to clean those lenses, we keep mistaking the filter for the truth.

That's the irony: we think we're seeing the world, but in truth, we're only seeing our version of it.

Let's explore the tree metaphor from a different perspective and deep dive into this concept below.

A World of Perspectives

Imagine this: a single tree standing in the middle of a street.

A monk sits beneath it, eyes closed, immersed in meditation. For him, the tree is a sanctuary, a silent refuge from the chaos of the world.

A scientist stands nearby, explaining photosynthesis to a group of curious listeners. To her, the tree is a marvel of biology, a gateway to understanding life.

A poor man approaches, axe in hand, cutting its branches for firewood. To him, the tree is survival, a means to feed his family.

A filmmaker pauses with their camera, framing it for the perfect romantic shot. For them, the tree is a symbol a metaphor for something deeper, perhaps love or eternity.

The tree remains the same. Yet, in the eyes of each observer, it transforms into something entirely different.

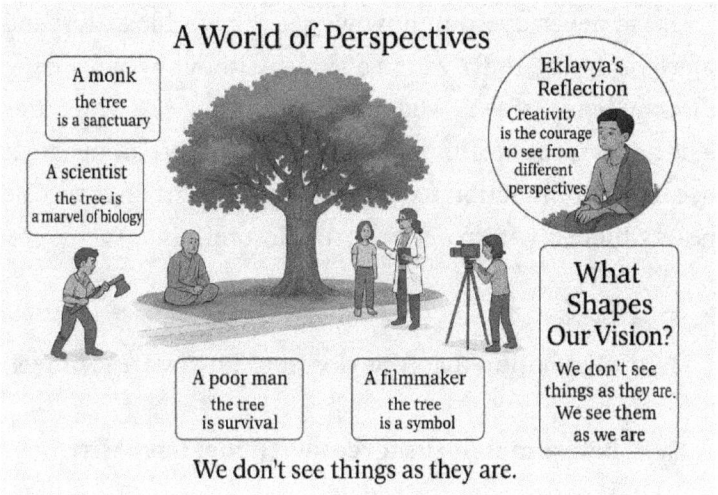

Figure 2: A World of Perspectives

Eklavya's Reflection

When Eklavya started questioning the way he saw things, people said he was overthinking. "Why complicate what's simple?" they'd say. But he couldn't stop. He had spent years watching people fight, struggle, and chase goals not because the world was wrong, but because their vision was never truly their own.

Over time, he realized something that changed him forever. Creativity isn't just about making art or solving problems it's the courage to see the same thing from different perspectives. It's the ability to build a vision that's uniquely yours, while still allowing space for other's perspectives to enrich it.

If we never question how we see the world, we'll spend our lives trying to fix what's outside, without ever realizing that the lens inside is what needs adjusting. And when our lens is clear, the world becomes more than just an image, it becomes an invitation to explore the truth, to discover the beauty hidden within even the simplest things.

Exercises:
Mark the option that feels closest to how you see or feel:

1. When someone disagrees with me, I usually:
a) Feel personally attacked
b) Try to explain my side
c) Pause to understand their point
d) Avoid the conversation

2. When I enter a new place or group, I often:
a) Feel judged or uncomfortable
b) Try to blend in quickly
c) Observe silently
d) Feel curious and open

3. When someone praises me, I tend to think:
a) They're just being polite
b) They mean it
c) What do they want from me?
d) I'm not sure what to believe

Visual Reflection Prompt:

Pick an object around you-a cup, a book, or the sun. Now, think: How do you see it? What are your feelings about these? What is the significance of it in your life?

By looking at historical examples, we will discover the power of vision in the next chapter.

4

The Power of Vision in History and Leadership

*****

"Leadership is the capacity to translate vision into reality."- **Warren Bennis**

Eklavya's Reflection

Eklavya sat by the window, the cool night air brushing against his face. The world outside was quiet, but inside his mind, a storm raged. That week, he had read about two men: Mahatma Gandhi and Adolf Hitler. Two leaders who had shaped history. Two men who had commanded unwavering loyalty. Two forces that had moved entire nations. They lived in the same century.

But their paths were so divergent.

Gandhi envisioned a world where peace was the answer. His strength lay in non-violence, in unshakable belief, in the power of people standing together without raising a single weapon.

Hitler, on the other hand, saw domination as his destiny. His vision was built on fear, on the need to control, on the belief that power came from crushing others beneath his feet.

Both had vision.

But that night, Eklavya realized something that unsettled him—vision alone was never enough.

Because what truly mattered was where that vision was rooted.

What History Tells Us?

If you trace back any great movement, any invention, any revolution you will always end up in the same place: someone's vision.

A single person looked at the world and thought, *This is not enough.* And then they imagined something different. Something better. They didn't just believe in it themselves. They made others believe in it, too. History is filled with such visions both noble and destructive. Lord Ram had a vision of righteousness, of a world where truth and dharma led the way. Ravana, too, had a vision one of power, of conquest, of proving his might. Both were relentless in their pursuit. But their outcomes were defined by the foundation of their vision.

The truth is, whether we realize it or not, we are all living in a world built by the visions of those who came before us. The schools we attend, the jobs we work at, the laws we follow each one started as a thought in someone's mind.

And if their vision had the power to shape our reality, then ours can, too. The real question is not, *Do I have a vision?*

The real question is *What kind of world is my vision building?*

A Scene to Imagine:

Picture this: You stand at a crossroads. Two roads stretch out before you. One leads to peace, dignity, and long-term growth. It's steady, sometimes slow, but built on strong, unshakable ground. The other promises control, speed, and surface success. It shines bright at first, tempting you with quick wins, but its foundation is shaky. At the starting point, both roads seem similar. Both are filled with opportunities. Both have challenges unexpected turns, steep climbs, and rough patches. But the true test?

The road you choose will define not just where you go, but who you become along the way.

Eklavya's Thought:

As a child, Eklavya had always dreamed of *doing something big*. He used to picture himself achieving great things, standing on grand stages, being known. But nobody ever asked him *Big for whom? Big in whose eyes?*

He had never asked himself either. Now, he understood. A vision without purpose is like a lamp without oil. It may flicker. It may even glow for a moment. But it will never light the path forward.

And he wanted his vision to do more than just shine. He wanted it to guide. To build. To last.

The Choice Before Us:

We all have vision, whether we realize it or not. The choices we make, the dreams we chase, the battles we pick—each one is shaped by the vision we hold in our minds.

The only thing that matters is whether that vision is leading us toward something greater or simply blinding us with momentary brilliance.

And so, Eklavya asked himself the only question that truly mattered:

Is my vision building a world I'd be proud to live in?

Exercises:

Mark the option that best reflects your response to the situation:

1. **When I see someone become successful, I usually think:**
   a) They must be lucky
   b) They must be well-connected
   c) They must have worked hard
   d) I want to know their journey

2. **When I look at my future, I feel:**
   a) I feel pressured to achieve something fast
   b) Confused about what I want
   c) Hopeful, even if unclear
   d) Clear about what kind of impact I want to make
3. **When I hear about a leader or public figure, I usually:**
   a) Get impressed by their power
   b) Wonder if they genuinely help others
   c) Compare them with myself
   d) Question what their core values are

Visual Reflection Prompt:

Imagine a fork in the road one path leads to personal success and comfort, and the other leads to collective impact without fame. Which path feels more aligned with your vision and why?

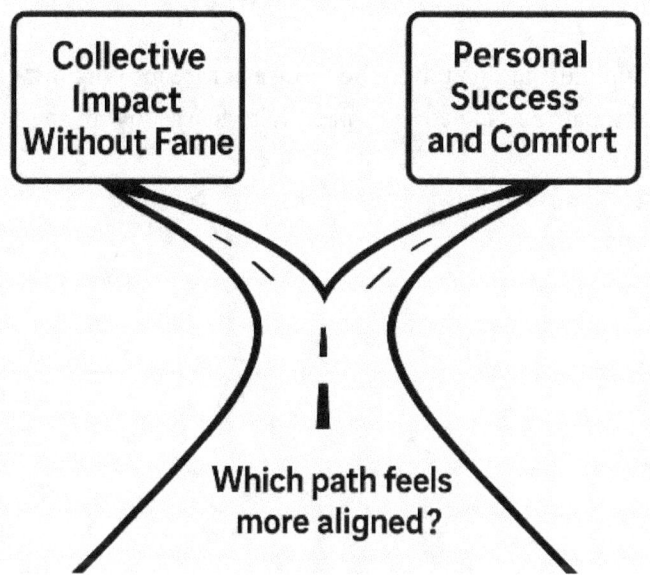

Figure 3: Fork in the Road

Path A: Personal Success	Path B: Collective Impact
Wealth, Fame, Comfort	Service, Humility, Legacy
Short-term gains	Long-term societal change
What can I achieve?	How can I uplift others?

| Aligned with ego | Aligned with compassion |

Table 1: Personal success versus collective impact

We must understand who we are before moving forward on the path of collective impact. Let's learn how in the next chapter.

5

Who am I?

*****

"To be yourself in a world that is constantly trying to make you something else is the greatest accomplishment." - **Ralph Waldo Emerson**

Eklavya sat on his porch, watching the world slow down as the evening crept in. The laughter of children playing nearby, the murmur of voices in the distance—it all felt familiar. Yet, tonight, familiarity felt less like home and more like a cage.

He thought back to his childhood, to the voices that had shaped him before he even knew himself.

"He looks just like his grandfather."

"He'll be like his father-calm and responsible."

"He's a tribal boy, but smart for his background."

At first, those words made him feel special. Like he had a place, a story already written for him. But as he grew older, they started feeling heavier. Like a jacket that never quite fit but one he was expected to wear forever.

How could so many people tell him who he was—before he had a chance to figure it out for himself?

What We Inherit Without Asking

We enter this world as blank pages, but before we can even pick up a pen, others begin writing our story for us. Family, culture, religion, society they all hand us pieces of an identity, a script we are expected to follow.

Without realizing it, we start adjusting ourselves to fit the roles we've been given. A daughter should behave this way. A son should act that way. This is what success looks like. This is what failure means.

We accept it because it's familiar. Because questioning it feels like breaking an unspoken rule.

But what if we don't fit the story we've been given? What if we want to write our own?

The Hidden Wall of Social Vision

Eklavya had always imagined society as a massive wall made of two kinds of bricks:

- **Vertical divisions**—gender, caste, religion, family status.
- **Horizontal divisions**—income, education, profession.

Everyone grows up between these walls. Some accept them, some break through. And some spend their whole lives wondering if there was ever a door.

There's a powerful force at play what he called **borrowed vision**. We don't just inherit a name or a home; we inherit a way of seeing the world. A way of seeing ourselves.

We copy dreams, relationships, ambitions not because they are right, but because they are **familiar**. And humans trust what they see often. That's how we survive in society. But that's also how we slowly lose the chance to see life through our own lens.

A Scene to Imagine:

Imagine a child walking into a room full of mirrors. In one, he sees his father's face staring back at him. In another, he's dressed like a priest, carrying the weight of faith. In another, he's wearing a school uniform, his future mapped out before him.

And then there's one mirror where he finally sees himself, just him. No labels, no expectations. Just the person he is, not the person he's been told to be.

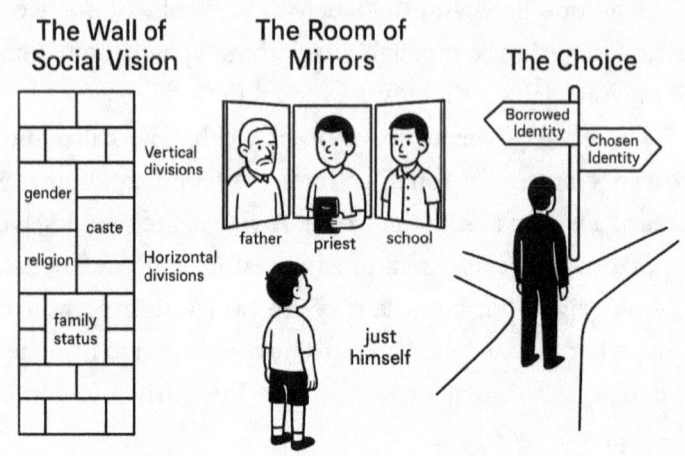

Figure 4: Breaking the Mirror

But as he reaches for that mirror, he hesitates. *Is he even allowed to choose this version of himself?*

Eklavya's Thought:

For the longest time, Eklavya wondered if he was living his life or the life others had imagined for him. Was he making choices for himself, or was he simply walking a path laid out by someone else long before he was born?

Now, he knew the answer:

A borrowed identity can only take you so far. But a chosen one? That can take you anywhere.

The Choice Before Us:

We all wear labels given to us by family, by society, by history. But at some point, we must ask ourselves:

If those labels didn't exist, who would I be?

Would I dream bigger? Would I walk a different path? Would I finally feel free to just be *me*?

Exercises:

Choose the option that best reflects how you see or feel:

1. When someone says I look or behave like a family member, I feel:

a) Proud and connected

b) Pressured to match with that identity

c) Question like this confused me

d) I don't care for such a question

2. When I hear someone talk about caste or religion while describing someone, I:

a) Accept it as norms

b) Feel uncomfortable but stay silent

c) Feel angry or frustrated

d) Try to see beyond that labels

3. When thinking about my childhood identity, I feel:

a) Grateful for the guidance

b) Limited by expectations

c) Confused about who I indeed was

d) I never thought deeply about it

Visual Reflection Prompt:

Think of one identity label others used for you based on looks, gender, background, or behaviour. Imagine how your life might look today if that label didn't exist. How would you do things differently if you could?

Who am I?, a question that has baffled humanity for thousands of years. The answer to this question clears all the murky waters around you. With this understanding, you move to the next level of life -one that helps you redefine the meaning of success. Let's learn about it in the next chapter.

6

Redefine the Meaning of Success

*****

*"Success is liking yourself, liking what you do, and liking how you do it."- **Maya Angelou***

Eklavya's Reflection

The train rattled along the tracks, a steady hum beneath my thoughts. I was staring out the window, watching the world blur by, when I struck up a conversation with a man sitting across from me. He looked to be in his late 40s, sharp in a pressed suit, his fingers flicking through business emails on his phone. His English was crisp, polished—like someone who'd spent years climbing ladders. He had the air of someone who had it all together, the kind of person you'd expect to have life figured out.

We exchanged the usual pleasantries—weather, delays, the little inconveniences of travel. But then, in a brief pause, he looked up from his screen, exhaled, and said, almost to himself, "I've done everything I was supposed to built the career, bought the house, earned the respect. But somewhere along the way, I lost track of why I was doing it."

His voice was steady, but there was a crack in it. I didn't push him to explain. I didn't need to. I'd seen that same hollow look before, behind the polished smiles of so-called "successful" people. And truth be told, I'd felt it myself after finishing my degree, landing a stable job, even starting my own business. It feels like something isn't right, like we're stuck in a game that keeps going with no pause button.

From the time we're kids, we're told to aim high. Parents, teachers, everyone—they drill it into us. *Reach for the stars.* But no one stops to tell you what "high" actually means—or whose stars you're supposed to be chasing. We grow up in a world obsessed with what's visible: a fat paycheck, a shiny title, a house with a garage full of stuff. Success gets measured in numbers and nods from other people. Failure? That's the whispers—the raised eyebrows when you take a gap year, switch paths, or dare to sit still for a minute. *She didn't make it. He's fallen behind.* But those definitions? They're not rooted in anything real. They're just a script, handed to us like a playbook we're supposed to follow without asking why.

And when life doesn't match that script—when the boxes in front of the goal don't get ticked in the right order. This quiet panic, like we're losing a race we didn't even sign up for.

It starts early, doesn't it? The labels. They creep into family dinners, spill out at reunions, stick to us like damp clothes. *"He's the first engineer in the family,"* someone boasts, and you can hear the pride swelling. *"She couldn't clear the exam again,"* another voice mutters, and the pity stings sharper than any failure ever could. *"They're doing well—just bought a new car,"* as if four wheels prove you've cracked the code. *"He left his job—must not be doing great,"* and suddenly a bold choice turns into a warning.

We carry those words around like weights. They sink into us, deeper than we realize, until one day we catch ourselves staring in the mirror, and ask these questions:

Not *Am I happy?*

Not *Do I love what I'm doing?*

Not even *Am I growing?*

Instead, we must ask:

Whether I change the life of the people around me?

Is the growth I envisioned helping others along the way?

And that shift us.

I've watched it play out everywhere. Students grinding for degrees they hate, their eyes dull, because it's what their parents dreamed for them Professionals stay in jobs they dislike because change feels like failure. People chasing more-more money, more status, more stuff-without ever stopping to enjoy the pile they've already built. It's exhausting just to watch. Like they're all sprinting after a bus that's not even headed where they want to go, but they keep running because everyone else is.

Eklavya's Thought:

I've seen the other side, too. Farmers who work sunrise to sunset, hands rough and backs bent, but they sleep peacefully. CEOs who command boardrooms and bank accounts, yet lie awake at night, restless, chasing a peace they can't buy. Students with perfect scores cry for more whereas artists, despite having little money, glow with passion for their work. It's not about what's in your hands. It's about what's in your chest—how close you feel to the path you're walking.

Success shouldn't be a label slapped on you by someone else. It's a feeling. A quiet knowing that you're where you're meant to be.

Picture this: a school assembly hall, buzzing with parents and kids. A boy steps up to the podium, a gold medal dangling from his neck. The crowd claps, loud and proud, cameras flashing. But when he looks up, his eyes are blank—distant, like he's not even there. He'd trained for months, nailed every test, but the weight of that medal feels heavier than the victory. A few rows back, another boy sits empty-handed. No prize, no spotlight. He'd spent weeks building a project he loved—a messy, imperfect thing that didn't win. But he's grinning, cheeks flushed with a kind of joy that spills over. He'd poured himself into something that mattered to him, and that was enough.

So tell me—who walked away the real winner that day?

Figure 5: From Illusion to Inner Fulfillment

Exercises:

Choose the option that most reflects your inner response or situation:

1. When I think of success, the first thing that comes to mind is:

a) Money and career growth
b) Social respect or family pride
c) Inner satisfaction and peace
d) A mix of things I haven't figured out yet

2. When I face failure or rejection, I usually:
a) Feel ashamed or judged
b) Try to ignore it
c) Reflect and try to grow
d) Compare myself with others who seem more stable

3. When I see others achieving things I don't have, I:
a) I Feel inspired
b) I Feel pressured
c) Question my own path
d) Remind myself that everyone's timeline is different

Visual Reflection Prompt:

Draw or list three things you've achieved that the world doesn't see or talk about—something you're quietly proud of.

Now ask yourself: What would my life look like if I celebrated these and more?

You begin to define your own success when you shift your focus from external validation to personal fulfillment and that happens when you aligned your life with purpose, impact, and joy.

Taking the next step on the ladder of fulfillment requires breaking the chain of conformity. Let's learn how to do this in the next chapter.

7

Breaking the Chains of Conformity

*****

*"You don't become what you want. You become what you believe."- **Oprah Winfrey***

Eklavya's Reflection

I remember gazing up at those towering institutions. Schools, offices, colleges, temples, even the military – they loomed large, radiating an aura of power and purpose. Giants, they seemed. Places where lives took shape and dreams found their footing. You felt the awe too, didn't you? It seems that they held some vital key, some secret to unlocking life's mysteries.

But then, you started noticing the cracks. Not in the bricks and mortar, but in the very souls of the places. Students, their curiosity stifled and they afraid to ask the questions burning in their minds. Employees chasing results instead of chasing passions, their individuality slowly fading. Worshippers silence their doubts, burying questions under layers of doctrine. Soldiers marching in perfect unison, but their critical thinking sacrificed at the altar of obedience.

Tell me, did those places nurture their spirits, or did they merely confine them?

And here's the crucial question, the one that might make you shift uncomfortably in your seat: Are you letting those invisible walls confine you, too?

Don't mistake compliance for purpose. Don't mistake silence for agreement. Don't mistake obedience for fulfillment.

Break the mold. Question the giants. Challenge the status quo. Dare to carve your own path. Your spirit – your unique, brilliant, beautiful spirit – deserves nothing less.

How it Begins:

Every institution starts with a spark—a goal, a dream, a reason. Take a school: it's born to teach, to open minds. An office rises to build something new and dream for flow of creativity. A temple promises peace or truth. At first, there's energy, change, a rush of possibility. But then the rules creep in. Structure hardens.

Imagine yourself as a river, serene and free-flowing. A dam obstructs your course, diverting your waters for power and control. The pent-up energy, denied its natural path, seeks release, culminating in an earthquake.

That's what I see now. Schools, the military, and companies, in their pursuit of rankings, discipline, and performance, often overlook the individual. It's not about shaping us anymore—it's about standardizing us. Making sure we all fit the mold. And in that process, they sand down the edges:

1) Creativity gets boxed in. 2) Questions get a stern look. 3) Silence wins over speaking up. 4)Genuine emotions get suppressed.

Figure 6: The Institutional Paradox

Most of us bend to it. But a few—they push back. The rebels, the outliers, the ones who don't fit. They're the ones who refuse to let their vision shrink, even when the world calls them troublemakers.

Eklavya's Thought

Let's pull apart the places we don't question enough. Start with schools. I remember sitting in class, pencil scratching, memorizing dates and formulas. But no one taught me *how* to think—just *what* to think. Risk-taking? Leadership? Figuring out who I was? Nah, that wasn't on the syllabus. It was all about the marks—your golden ticket. But a ticket to where? No one said.

Then college. They'd slap "dream big" on every poster, but the reality? Placements, paychecks, and skills that barely scratched the surface. Research, innovation, building something for the world.

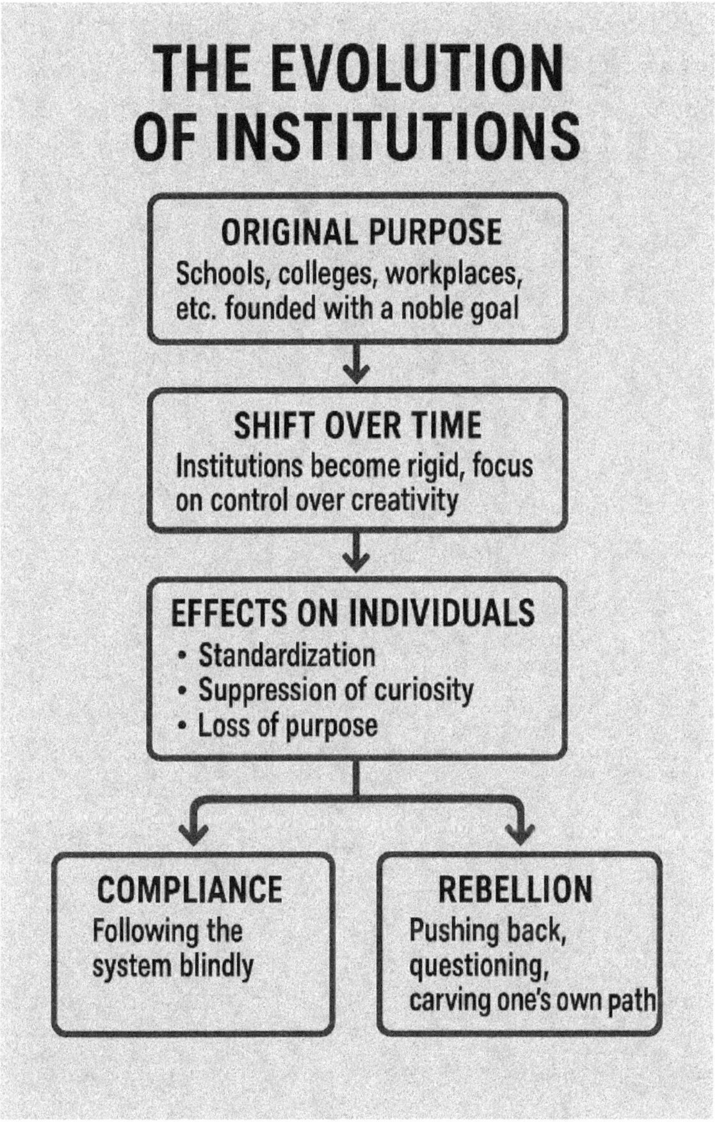

THE EVOLUTION OF INSTITUTIONS

ORIGINAL PURPOSE
Schools, colleges, workplaces, etc. founded with a noble goal

⬇

SHIFT OVER TIME
Institutions become rigid, focus on control over creativity

⬇

EFFECTS ON INDIVIDUALS
- Standardization
- Suppression of curiosity
- Loss of purpose

⬇

COMPLIANCE
Following the system blindly

REBELLION
Pushing back, questioning, carving one's own path

Figure 7: Control vs. Creativity

There's a chaos outside and it seems that everyone is living a scripted life and making you lose your inner voice. You find it (your inner voice) once you declutter this chaos. Let's learn how to do this in the next chapter.

8

Finding Your Voice in a Noisy World

*****

"We think we are making choices, but often we are just following the closest circle we belong to." - **Unknown**

Eklavya's Reflection

There was a time when asking for advice meant walking up to someone older, someone wiser maybe your parent, your teacher, your neighbour. You'd sit with them, face to face, and listen.

Now? We ask our group chats.

WhatsApp, Instagram DMs, or the latest reel screaming advice with the background music. We're swimming in opinions but still thirsty for clarity.

And strangely, we're lonelier than ever.

Eklavya stood in the middle of a crowded room. The lights were bright, the music pulsed through the floor, and laughter echoed from every corner. People moved with confidence, their clothes sharp, their smiles curated like Instagram grids. Each voice around him buzzed with advice, opinions, trends, and noise.

"Be more assertive," one said. "Try this filter it'll make your skin glow," another laughed. "Don't waste your time on that dream. It's not practical," chimed someone else. "Go viral. That's the only way to matter."

Figure 8: Listen to the Original Sound Within You

The voices weren't just around him. They were inside him echoes from reels he'd seen, posts he'd liked, and comments he'd read without noticing how deeply they etched themselves into his being. He looked around and realized... no one here really knew him. And more hauntingly, he wasn't sure he knew himself either.

For a moment, the lights flickered, and the room blurred like a paused video. In that pause, he felt a different voice quieter, unsure, but warm.

"What do you want?"

It wasn't loud. It didn't demand attention. But it was his. A voice from a time before likes and shares. Before opinions became currency. Before identity became performance.

His chest tightened with a strange mix of grief and relief. Grief for the parts of himself he had muted to fit in. Relief that something real still lived beneath the noise.

He stepped back, trying to tune in again. The louder voices protested, growing more urgent, more frantic. But he just stood there, eyes closed, letting the quiet rise like a slow tide.

A tear slipped down his cheek not out of sadness, but from the sheer tenderness of remembering himself.

In a world that rewards echoes, he chose to listen to the original sound within him.

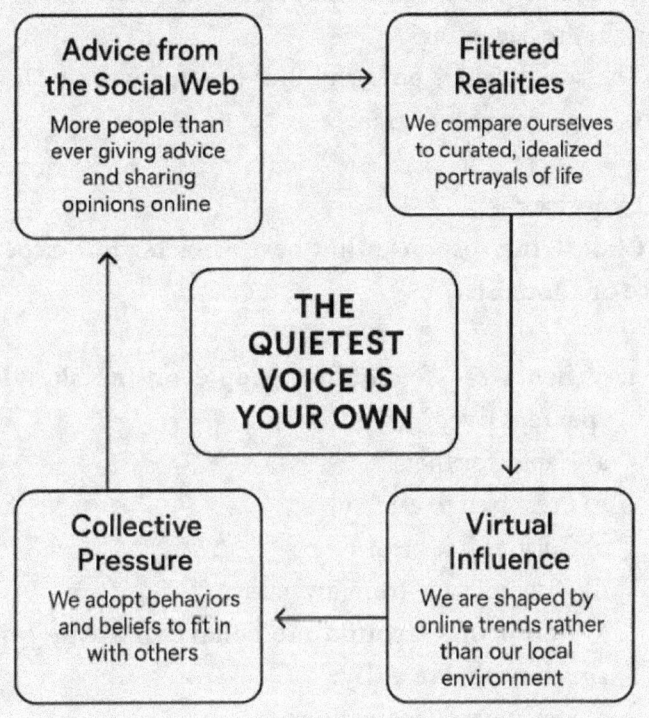

Figure 9: Cycle of Echoes

Eklavya's Thought:

Sometimes, I wonder if the internet went silent for just one month.

Would people still know who they are?

Would they know what they like, what they believe in, who they're becoming?

The social web is powerful. But like any web, it can do two things: connect or trap.

Exercises:

Choose the response that best reflects your experience or thoughts:

1. **When I see friends or people online showing "perfect lives," I feel:**
   a) Happy for them
   b) Pressured to catch up
   c) Curious if it's real
   d) Disconnected from my path
2. **When people around me behave in a way I disagree with, I usually:**
   a) Stay quiet to maintain peace
   b) Feel alone but don't express
   c) Try to understand both sides
   d) Speak up or quietly step away
3. **When I spend a lot of time online, I feel:**
   a) Entertained and Informed
   b) Distracted and unfocused

c) Inspired but confused
d) Tired and emotionally low

Visual Reflection Prompt:

Think about your closest circle-family, friends, and online community. Draw or describe how each influences your opinions, choices, and feelings.
Now ask: Are these influences making me more authentic or more confused?

Let's go to the next chapter that discusses the mirror that never speaks the truth. Don't forget-your reality, your story, is the truth. The mirror the world shows you isn't meant for you."

9

The Mirror Is Not the Truth

*****

"We live in a world where perception sells better than truth."-
Unknown

Eklavya's Reflection

There was a time when I believed in heroes on screens. The kind who stood alone, fists clenched, backlit by explosions or swelling background music changing the world in under three hours. The heroes always looked like gods, never tired, never confused. Always sure. Always right.

I admired them. We all did.

But admiration has a shadow it makes you wonder if you're too small, too ordinary to matter.

Then I grew up. And the real heroes looked different. Some had worn-out shoes. Some came home late to tired children. Some showed up every day for others, without applause, cameras, or hashtags. They weren't fighting wars. They were holding spaces. Teaching. Healing. Listening.

Not to millions, but to two or three people. And yet, their impact was deep because it was real.

That's when it hit me.

The world I saw wasn't the world that exists.

It was the version someone wanted me to see.

And I began to ask: *Who's holding the camera? Who's editing the frame?*

The Manufactured Mirror

In today's world, media isn't just a storyteller. It's a sculptor of perception. From TV anchors to trending reels, from film scripts to influencer captions—we are told:

Who to admire.

What to chase.

Who to hate.

What to buy.

And more dangerously-*who we are.*

But here's the truth:

The lens we're looking through is often sponsored, strategised, or manipulated.

Celebrities speak on justice—but only during a brand campaign.

Influencers post about authenticity with a carefully edited background. Movies build dreams but on sets.

And we?

We start following performances, comparing ourselves to characters.

The Power of Repetition:

Repeat anything enough, and it becomes belief. So when media repeatedly shows:

- Fair skin equals beauty
- Wealth equals worth
- Loudness equals leadership
- Strength equals suppression
- Certain communities as villains

We don't just consume it. We begin to carry it.

We carry these beliefs into our workplaces, into classrooms, into homes, into mirrors. And worse-we forget they weren't even ours.

Culture or Content?

Culture once came from shared life. From the wisdom of elders, from rituals that brought people together, from stories told at night without screens.

Now, it comes from algorithms.

Our weddings become content.

Our grief becomes posts.

Our kindness becomes PR.

And slowly, invisibly, our vision becomes external.

We begin to ask not "How do I feel?" but "How do I look?"

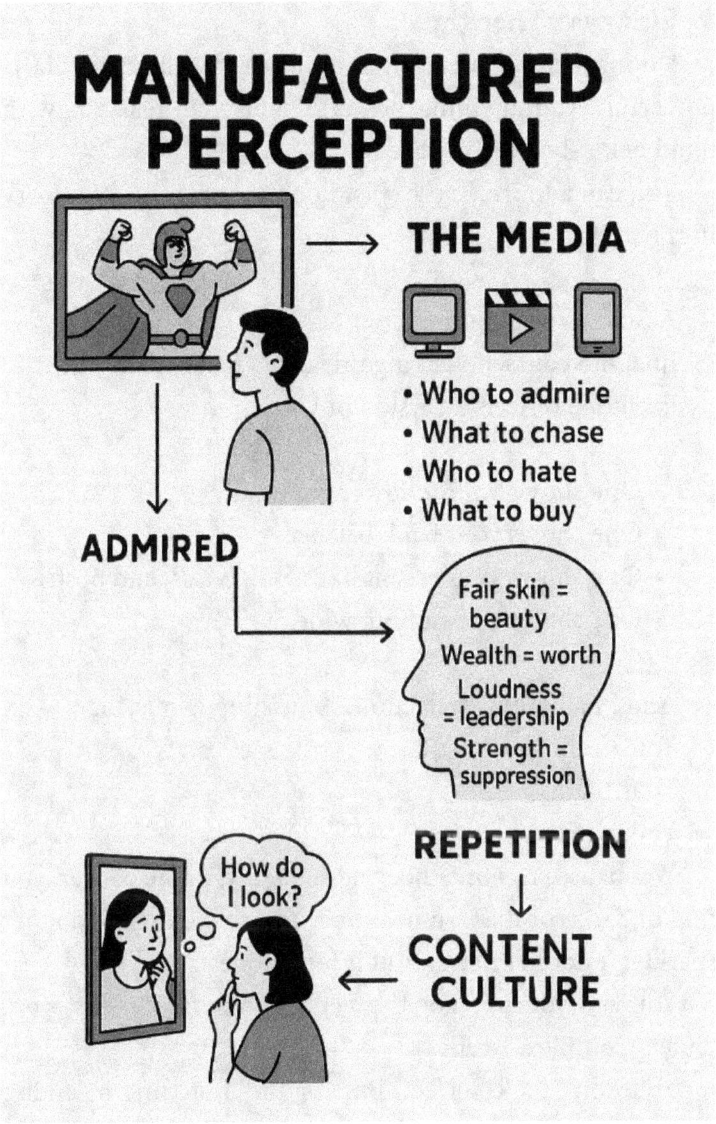

MANUFACTURED PERCEPTION

THE MEDIA

- Who to admire
- What to chase
- Who to hate
- What to buy

ADMIRED

Fair skin = beauty

Wealth = worth

Loudness = leadership

Strength = suppression

REPETITION

↓

CONTENT CULTURE

How do I look?

Figure 10: The Illusions of Perception

Eklavya's Thought:

I don't believe media is the villain. I believe media is powerful. And anything powerful must be held-not with blind belief-but with awareness.

You can admire a hero. Just don't forget your own story in the process.

A Scene to Imagine:

Imagine yourself walking through a hall of mirrors.
Each one reflects a version of you:

- One shows your follower count.
- One shows your bank balance.
- One shows your recent likes, purchases, and posts.
- One shows you smiling wide.

And in all of this reflection, something is missing.
Your feeling.
Your truth.
Your silence.

You pause. You breathe. And suddenly, in the corner, you find one mirror dusty, untouched. You step closer. It doesn't sparkle. It doesn't flatter. But it feels honest.

You see yourself not the version others see. Just you. Quiet. Complex. Real.

You don't look perfect. But for the first time in a long time, you recognise yourself.

Exercises:

Choose the response that best reflects your thoughts or experience:

1. When I watch celebrities or influencers online, I usually feel:

a) Inspired by their lifestyle

b) Curious about their real life

c) Pressured to look or live like them

d) Detached—I know it's a show

2. When I see a product or idea repeated often in media, I:

a) Feel drawn to try or believe it

b) Wonder who is behind it

c) Ignore it unless I need it

d) Start questioning the intention

3. When I think about how media shapes perception, I feel:

a) Aware but still affected

b) Distracted and influenced

c) Clear and alert

d) Unsure what to trust anymore

Visual Reflection Prompt:

List or draw three "media-created" ideas you used to believe and it can be about beauty, success, love, career, or happiness.

Now ask: Where did those ideas come from and do they still serve me?

Like Eklavya, we've all lived with a certain murkiness, a fog obscuring our vision, haven't we? His dilemmas, struggles, and searching are reflections of our own. But what if you could wipe away the dirt, polish the lens of your perception? This book now offers you the tools, the strategies, the power to see life with stunning clarity in the next phase of the book. Are you ready to redesign it?

SECTION TWO

DESIGN YOUR DESTINY

"You cannot go back and change the beginning. But you can start from where you are and change the ending."
*- **C.S. Lewis***

10

Introduction to Part Two

*****

"The challenge lies not in simply following our feelings, but in knowing which feelings to trust."- **Alain de Botton**

So far, we've uncovered the many layers that silently shape how we see the world-family, school, society, media, and history. Each of these forces, in their own way, hands us a lens. And over time, without even realizing it, we begin to look through that lens as if it were the only one that exists.

But here's the truth: those lenses can limit us. They can become narrow, borrowed, or even broken.

Now comes the question that can shift everything - Can we design a new vision for ourselves?

The answer is a resounding yes.

But this isn't about tearing everything down.

It's not about blaming our past or pointing fingers at the systems that shaped us.

It's about something deeper. Braver.

It's about choosing to live with intention.

It takes courage to question what we've always known. Confidence to trust our inner voice.

It takes acceptance, of both our wounds and our wisdom. And above all, it takes the willingness to see the world-not just as it is-but as it *could be*.

We need more than just dreams.

We need a living vision.

One that helps us design a life aligned with who we are, not just who we were told to be.

Let's be clear-beliefs, systems, traditions, cultures-they aren't the enemy.

They were built for a reason. Some still hold wisdom.

But the problem begins when these things become frozen in time.

When they stop evolving. When they stop listening.

When they forget that their purpose is to serve people-not control them.

Any true system, any real culture worth preserving, should make every person feel like they matter. Like they belong. Like they can grow-and eventually, help others grow too.

That's how we build a generation of leaders. Not followers.

Not rebels without roots-but pioneers with purpose.

So in this part of the journey, we will explore how to:

- Let go of what no longer serves us
- Add new meaning to what already exists
- Create a living vision-rooted in clarity, flexibility, and inner truth

This isn't about escaping your life.
It's about *realigning* with it.
It's about finding that sacred balance between what you want, how you want to live, and who you are becoming.

Because when you live with vision, you don't just survive.
You come alive.

Let's explore different steps to help you redesign your life in the next three chapters.

11

Redesigning the Inner Lens

*****

"You carry worlds within you—not all your own. To find yourself, lay down the borrowed, the unasked, the unseen chains. Then, and only then, will you walk as the river does: free, yet purposeful."- **Kahlil Gibran**

Eklavya's Reflection
When I truly began to reflect on my life, I realized I wasn't just carrying memories—I was carrying patterns. Habits passed down like heirlooms. Definitions I never questioned. Fears that weren't even mine.

I was still responding like the schoolboy I once was. Still trying to prove myself like the young man who had left his tribal town behind to make a name in the city.

None of it was wrong.
But some of it… was no longer me.

So I started the quiet process of unlearning.
And strangely, that's when the real learning began.

Step 1: Acknowledge What's Already Shaped You

Before you can redesign your vision, you must meet the one you're currently living with—honestly, without filters.

Ask yourself:

- Who taught me what success looks like?
- Who made me believe failure was something to fear?
- Whose voice echoes in my head when I feel guilty, unsure, or not enough?

This isn't about blame.

This is about clarity.

You cannot change what you cannot name.

Step 2: Clear the Lens

We all wear a lens—crafted by years of judgments, comparisons, and silent assumptions.

It shapes how we see others, and how we think they see us.

Clean that lens—not with aggression, but with curiosity.

Look at people as stories, not stereotypes.

Look at yourself with gentleness, not shame.

If you don't understand someone yet—stay. Ask. Listen.

Growth doesn't shout. It whispers. And it waits.

Step 3: Become a Student of Life

Life is your best teacher—but only if you remain a humble student.

Observe people around you:

- Those who seem peaceful, not just successful.
- Those who live simply, but fully.
- Those who are present, even in silence.

They may not be famous. They may not have perfect answers.
But if their light touches something in you—follow it for a while.

Speak to them.
Ask questions without trying to sound smart.
Let them challenge your beliefs.
Let their stories soften your judgments.

Learning begins when the need to impress disappears.

Step 4: Prototype Before You Permanently Change

Don't try to transform your life overnight.
Instead, **prototype** your growth.

- Try one new habit for 7 days.
- Read one new perspective and apply it to one area of your life.
- Test. Observe. Adjust.

If it resonates—keep going.

If it doesn't—tweak, don't quit.

You don't find your vision in a single leap.

You refine it, like a sculptor, one gentle stroke at a time.

Step 5: Make Learning a Lifestyle

Transformation isn't an event it's a rhythm.

Build your rhythm:

- Read books that stretch, not just comfort you.
- Find mentors you can trust deeply. Keep them close.
- Journal your insights—not to post, but to remember.
- Sit with your thoughts like they're friends.
- Create a ladder of learning—some mentors close, some distant, some in books, some in real life.

Repeat this cycle like the seasons. Let your life bloom again and again.

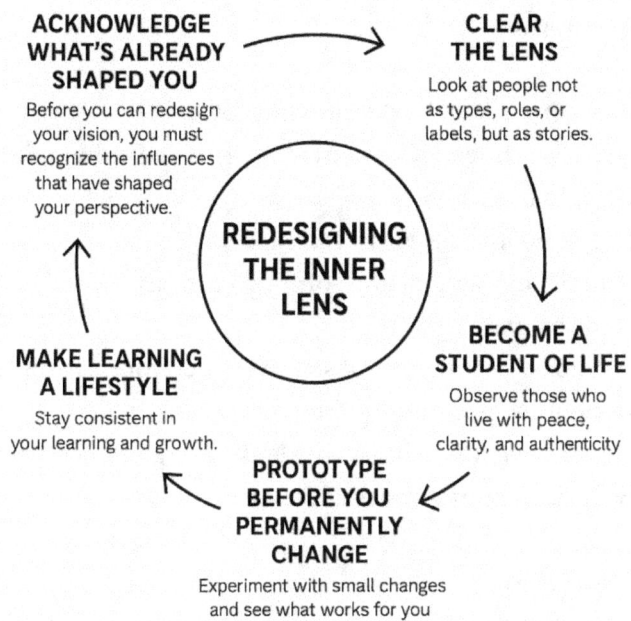

Figure 11: The 5-Step Journey to Redesigning Your Vision

Eklavya's Thought:

I've stopped chasing grand answers.
Now, I chase small shifts:

A better question.
A deeper conversation.
A new morning habit.

We grow faster in the presence of people we trust and admire. So choose your circle with care.Be humble. Be grateful. Express love.
Balance both success and satisfaction.
Be bold in your action, and soft in your heart.
And remember:
Life is not a destination. It's a river. Let your vision flow with it not by force, but by trust.
That's how you redesign the lens through which you see the world. By seeing yourself... clearly.

Exercises:

Choose the response that fits your current experience or emotion:

1. When I look at my past beliefs, I feel:

a) Grateful, but ready to let some go
b) Conflicted and stuck
c) Curious about where they came from
d) Unsure if they were ever really mine

2. When I meet someone who challenges my usual way of thinking, I:

a) Listen and reflect
b) Feel uncomfortable or defensive
c) Avoid deeper conversations
d) Ask more questions to understand

3. When I try something new (a habit, routine, idea), I usually:
   a) Stick with it and observe
   b) Give up if it doesn't feel right fast
   c) Keep adjusting until it fits
   d) Compare it with others before accepting

Visual Reflection Prompt:

Draw or list three beliefs you want to unlearn. Then, write one sentence for each:

Why it no longer serves you?

What you want to replace it with?

12

The Vision Within

*****

*"Your time is limited, so don't waste it living someone else's life. Don't be trapped by dogma — which is living with the results of other people's thinking."- **Steve Jobs***

Eklavya's Reflection

When I began unlearning, something unexpected happened
I didn't just feel lighter.
I began to notice **gaps.**
In how I worked.
In the kind of relationships I was in.
In how I defined success, failure, happiness even peace.

But here's the twist:
Those gaps didn't scare me anymore.
They gave me **space.**

Space to breathe.
Space to imagine.
Space to ask a question I had never dared to before:
What would my life look like if I designed it from within-not borrowed it from the world outside?

Why Designing Matters?

We spend so much of our lives trying to **fit** into systems, into roles, into labels, into expectations.

We master the art of adjusting. But somewhere along the way, we stop asking:

"What do I actually want to build?"

The truth is you already have a vision.

Even if it's not yet clear. It whispers through your daydreams, hides in your frustrations, shines in your moments of admiration, and sits quietly in your silent wishes.

This chapter is about turning that quiet whisper into a **clear, living framework.** Something you can shape, share, and walk with.

Step 1: Observe What Bothers You

Sometimes, your vision is hiding inside your irritations. Ask yourself:

- What do I often complain about?
- What problems make me restless?
- What gaps do I see in how people live, work, or connect?

These aren't just annoyances.
They are **clues**—markers from your inner compass, nudging you toward what matters.

Your vision doesn't always begin with a dream. Sometimes, it starts with discomfort.

Step 2: Ask, "What Would I Do Differently?"
Now take a look around.
Pick any broken system—education, relationships, the way we work or treat nature.

And ask:

- How would I redesign this, if no one could stop me?
- What would I add, remove, simplify, or rebuild?

Let your imagination flow.
Not for approval. Not for perfection.
Just for the **possibility**.

This is how your **creative blueprint** begins to form.

Step 3: Reimagine Growth Your Way
Step away from the noise.
Forget what growth looks like on reels or resumes.
Now ask:

- What does real growth mean to me?
- Is it peace? Freedom? Impact? Depth? Learning?
- What does progress **feel like**, not just **look like**?

Design your growth like a rhythm—not a race.
Let it be steady, soulful, even slow.
Because maybe your success is **quiet and deep**, not loud and fast.

Let it be **yours**.

Step 4: Map Your Vision
Now, gently and honestly, write it out:

1. What do I want to feel more of in my life?
2. What kind of people, projects, and places bring out the best in me?
3. What does my ideal day or week look like—balanced, not idealised?
4. What values do I want to honour every day?

These answers are your compass. Whenever you're lost, **come back here**.

Step 5: Add Your Lens to the World
Everything you see—career paths, cultures, success stories—
was once someone else's **version**.

Now, it's your turn.

- See what exists
- Honour what works
- Question what doesn't
- Add your layer

- Leave your mark

This is what vision truly is.
Not escape. Not imitation. It's a creation.

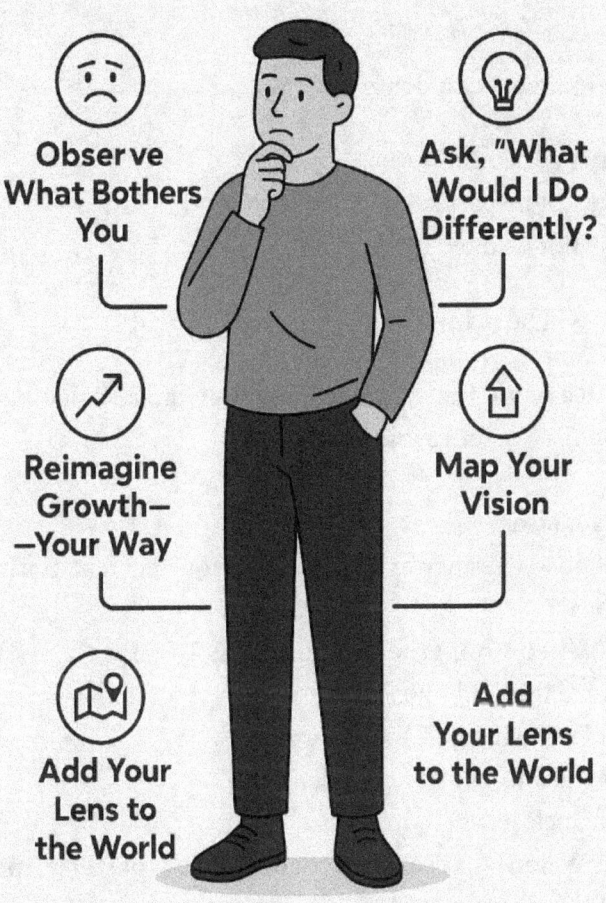

Figure 12: Designing from Within

Eklavya's Thought:

I used to think I had to choose a path that already existed. That I had to walk someone else's road just to reach somewhere valid.

Now I know-**I can draw my own**.

It may not be fast.
It may not be perfect.
It may not be liked by everyone.

But it will be **mine**.

And in a world that keeps handing us templates that kind of vision…is a quiet revolution.

Exercises:

Choose the answer that reflects your current clarity or response:

1. When I imagine designing my life, I feel:
a) Excited and open
b) Overwhelmed and unsure
c) Curious but not confident
d) Unclear where to start

2. When I observe a problem or pattern in the world, I often:
a) Think of ways to change it
b) Feel helpless to fix it
c) Wish someone else would solve it
d) Avoid thinking about it too much

3. My idea of growth involves:
a) Impact and contribution
b) Stability and balance
c) Freedom and exploration
d) Recognition and status

Visual Reflection Prompt:

Draw or describe your ideal day, week, or month. What are you doing? Who are you with? How do you feel at the end of it?

Then ask: What one small step can I take today to move toward that life?

13

The Seed and the Soil

*****

*"One day you will wake up and there won't be any more time to do the things you've always wanted. Do it now." - **Paulo Coelho***

Eklavya's Reflection

There was a time when my head was filled with brilliant thoughts. Ideas sparkled like stars but they remained up there, distant and untouchable.

I kept waiting...
For the perfect timing.
For the right version of me.
For a plan so flawless it would guarantee no mistakes.

It never came.

Then one day, I acted not with certainty, but with courage. I started with the miniature version. The unpolished one. The step that made my heart race. That day, something shifted. My vision stopped being a thought and began becoming a path.

Why Action Is the Final Step of Vision

You can read, plan, visualise, and dream. But until it touches your calendar, your habits, your wallet, your conversations- it stays a hope, not a reality.

It's not perfection that builds momentum it's motion.
A few small, bold steps repeated with intention can shape an entirely new life.

When your thoughts fuel your actions, and your actions refine your thoughts, you create a loop of power- the vision-action feedback cycle.

Figure 13: Vision-Action Feedback Cycle

Step 1: Create a Short-Term Vision (Just 2–3 Steps)

Long-term dreams are powerful, but too distant to act on.

Start small. Start real.

- Choose **one** area of your life-career, relationships, health, or purpose.
- Define the next **2–3 practical steps** you can take *this week*.
- Write it down. Place it where your eyes meet it daily.

Don't aim to "fix your life." **Activate it.**

Step 2: Feel the Future Before It Arrives

Your nervous system doesn't respond to words it responds to emotion.

- Close your eyes. **See yourself doing the thing**.
- How do you feel? What discomfort arises? What resistance?
- If you **fail**-how would you respond without shame?
- If you **succeed**-what does it feel like in your body?

This is not fantasy. It's **emotional rehearsal**—a way to familiarise your body with the unknown.

Step 3: Accept the Flow of Wins and Losses

Most people don't stop because they failed.
They stop because they mistook failure for the end.
But remember:

- Failure is **feedback**, not final.
- Delay is **design**, not denial.
- Setbacks are **signposts**, not stop signs.

Write this on your wall:
"My vision is not fragile. I am allowed to bend without breaking."

Step 4: Align Career, Money, and Purpose

Career, income, and impact don't always align together- but with intentional design, they can coexist.

Ask yourself:

- What kind of work makes me feel **alive**?
- What kind of work pays my bills with **dignity**?
- What kind of work brings **value to others**?

Your **sweet spot** lives at the intersection. You may not land there today. But every project, job, and conversation can be a **bridge**.

Step 5: Build a Vision Routine

Turn your vision into a daily practice, not a distant wish.
Here are a few things that can help you:

- Organise your thoughts.
- If your **actions** lack **intention**, pause and realign.
- If your **thoughts** lack **movement**, act.
- Learn. Act. Reflect. Repeat.
- Record and revisit.
- Accept. Celebrate. Continue.

The most meaningful visions are not executed in one burst.
They're nurtured—through quiet effort, deep presence, and persistent heart.

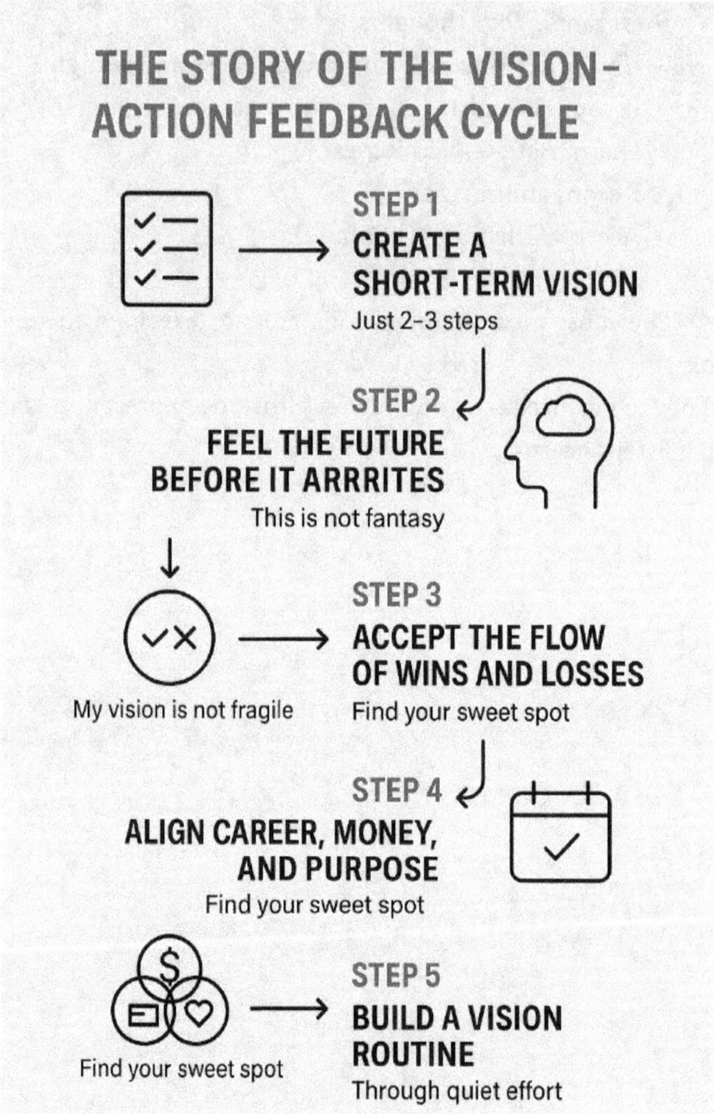

THE STORY OF THE VISION-ACTION FEEDBACK CYCLE

STEP 1
CREATE A SHORT-TERM VISION
Just 2–3 steps

STEP 2
FEEL THE FUTURE BEFORE IT ARRRITES
This is not fantasy

STEP 3
ACCEPT THE FLOW OF WINS AND LOSSES
Find your sweet spot

My vision is not fragile

STEP 4
ALIGN CAREER, MONEY, AND PURPOSE
Find your sweet spot

STEP 5
BUILD A VISION ROUTINE
Through quiet effort

Find your sweet spot

Figure 14: Steps of Vision-Action Cycle

Eklavya's Thought:

People tell me, "You're lucky you followed your passion."

What they don't see are the doubts I faced, the nights I stayed frozen, the fears I still carry.

I didn't build this life because I was **ready**.
I built it because I was **willing**.

A Scene to Imagine:

A person stands at the edge of a field.
In one hand, they hold a seed.
In the other—a perfect plan for growing a tree.
The plan is detailed, brilliant, step-by-step.

But unless that seed meets the soil…
Unless it faces sunlight, wind, rain, and seasons…
It remains only a **theory**.

Your ideas are seeds.
But **the soil is action**.

Plant something today. Even if it's small.
That's where the journey truly begins.

14

Conclusion: The World Is Yours to Design

*****

*"You are not a drop in the ocean. You are the entire ocean in a drop."- **Rumi***

The Journey from Vision to Reality

When we began this exploration, we asked a simple but profound question: Who is designing your world?

Now, as we reach the end, the answer is clear—you are.

Every belief you've questioned, every assumption you've challenged, and every small step you've taken has been an act of redesign. You've learned that vision is not just about seeing the world as it is, but shaping it as it could be.

The businessman chasing an elusive "more," the elderly woman content by the river, the cobbler who found meaning in every stitch—they all lived by different visions. And so do you. The difference now? You've chosen yours with intention.

The Three Truths to Carry Forward

1. Your Lens Shapes Your Life

- The world does not dictate your reality—your perception does.
- When you change how you see, you change how you live.

2. You Are Not Bound by Borrowed Beliefs

- Family, society, and media handed you a script.
- But you hold the pen to rewrite it.

3. Action Turns Vision into Legacy

- A dream remains a fantasy until it touches your habits, choices, and daily life.
- The smallest steps, taken consistently, build the grandest transformations.

A Final Invitation

This book is not an ending-it's a beginning. The real work starts now, in the quiet moments when you:

Pause before reacting, asking, "Is this truly my choice, or an old habit?"

Refuse to let fear, comparison, or borrowed expectations steer your path.

Create a life where success is defined by depth, not just applause.

You were born into a world designed by others. But the future? That's yours to shape. So go, design boldly, live authentically, and leave a mark only you can make.

The world is waiting.

Book References

1. **Angelou, M.** (1993). *Wouldn't take nothing for my journey now.* Random House.

2. **Bennis, W.** (1989). *On becoming a leader.* Addison-Wesley.

3. **Brown, B.** (2010). *The gifts of imperfection: Let go of who you think you're supposed to be and embrace who you are.* Hazelden.

4. **Csikszentmihalyi, M.** (1990). *Flow: The psychology of optimal experience.* Harper & Row.

5. **Duhigg, C.** (2012). *The power of habit: Why we do what we do in life and business.* Random House.

6. **Frankl, V. E.** (1946). *Man's search for meaning.* Beacon Press.

7. **Pink, D. H.** (2009). *Drive: The surprising truth about what motivates us.* Riverhead Books.

8. **Tolle, E.** (1999). *The power of now: A guide to spiritual enlightenment.* New World Library.

Recommended Reading For You

Unlearning & Identity

1. The Gifts of Imperfection – Brené Brown

2. The Four Agreements – Don Miguel Ruiz

3. Atomic Habits – James Clear

Social Vision & Systems

1. Sapiens – Yuval Noah Harari

2. Braiding Sweetgrass – Robin Wall Kimmerer

3. The Art of Thinking Clearly – Rolf Dobelli

Purpose & Action

1. Start with Why – Simon Sinek

2. Deep Work – Cal Newport

3. Essentialism – Greg McKeown

Mindset & Legacy

1. The Alchemist – Paulo Coelho

2. Let Your Life Speak – Parker J. Palmer

3. The River of Consciousness – Oliver Sacks

Notes:

Notes:

www.ingramcontent.com/pod-product-compliance
Lightning Source LLC
LaVergne TN
LVHW010553070526
838199LV00063BA/4962